Author:
Gerri Holden, M.S. Ed.

Editor:
Dona Herweck Rice

Editorial Project Manager:
Ina Massler Levin, M.A.

Editor-in-Chief:
Sharon Coan, M.S. Ed.

Illustrator:
Kathy Bruce

Cover Design:
Darlene Spivak

Cover Artist:
Sue Fullum

Art Director:
Elayne Roberts

Imaging:
Alfred Lau

Product Manager:
Phil Garcia

Publishers:
Rachelle Cracchiolo, M.S. Ed.
Mary Dupuy Smith, M.S. Ed.

STUDENTS
AGAINST
VIOLENCE

GRADES 1-5

Teacher Created Materials, Inc.
P.O. Box 1040
Huntington Beach, CA 92647

©1995 Teacher Created Materials, Inc.

Made in U.S.A.

ISBN-1-55734-518-X

Table of Contents

Teacher Directions 3

S.A.V. Membership Cards 6

Contract 7

Briefcase 8

Word Web 9

Hugs, Not Slugs 10

    Cloze Activity 11

    Handwriting Practice 12

    ABC Order 13

    What Do They Mean? 14

    Dictionary Skills 15

    Multiple Meanings 16

    Make a Word 17

    Synonym Search 18

Can You Solve a Mystery? 19

    Our Solutions 20

    Best Solutions 21

Let's Learn to Live Together 22

    Crack the Code 23

    Checklist 24

    Make a Better World 25

Secret Mission: The Year of the Child 26

    I Can Cope—I Don't Need Dope! 27

    I Know How to Handle "Stranger Danger" 28

    I'm Home Alone but Acting Grown 29

    Get a Grip! Gangs Aren't Hip 30

    Favorite Words 31

Literature: The Berenstain Bears 32

    Story Map I 33

    Story Map II 34

    Story Map III 35

    F. B. I. Book Report 36

    Bookmarks 37

Creative Writing 38

The Writing Process 39

Encyclopedia Search 40

Secret Language 41

Word Scramble 42

Newspaper Reporter 43

Student and Teacher Conference 45

Poster Contest 46

Special Diploma 47

Answer Key 48

Teacher Directions

1. **S.A.V. Membership Cards:** Have the students cut out the card (page 6) and fold it like a tent. After the students make their cards, advise them that as club members they can earn stickers. Here are some suggestions for what actions to reward:

   - sharing
   - peacefully resolving (not fighting)
   - saying kind words

   After the students have earned five stickers, give them a special treat.

2. **Contract:** Make copies of the contract (page 7) on colored paper. Each contract is to be completed by the student and the teacher.

3. **Briefcase:** Have the students follow the directions (page 8) to make briefcases, and if desired, they may also decorate them. Ask the students to store all their important documents (activity sheets) inside their briefcases.

4. **Word Web:** Ensure that the students understand the term "violence" by having them complete the word web (page 9). Discuss their work. If possible, have the students share and discuss their ideas in small groups.

   To use the worksheet, first give each student a copy or place it on the overhead. Discuss the meaning of the word "violence." Write down the students' responses. Then, have each student write a short story (or essay) about what violence is and why it is wrong. The students can include positive ways to solve problems, such as forgiving others, not being overly sensitive, talking problems over, seeking the help of an adult, learning self-control, and learning respect for others.

5. **Hugs, Not Slugs Rap:** Make a copy of the rap (page 10) for each student. To help them memorize the rap, have them complete pages 11, 12, 13, and 14. They can then share their rap with their families at home, and they can also perform the rap for the principal or other classes.

   To challenge your students, let them try "Make a Word" on page 17. The children can work in groups to come up with as many words as possible. Then, bring the class together again. On the chalkboard, list the words the students have found.

   Additional skill activities that use the rap can be found on pages 15, 16, and 18. Have the students follow the directions on those pages.

6. **Can You Solve a Mystery?:** Divide your class into cooperative learning groups. Give each group a copy of pages 19 and 20. As a discussion starter, direct the students to determine some reasons why people fight. If necessary, use some of the prompts below:

   - gang affiliation
   - uncontrolled anger
   - feelings of helplessness, sadness, or loneliness
   - unaware of a better way to solve problems

Once the students have discussed some of the reasons for violence, they must decide the best solution for solving the problem of violence. (Use page 20 for this exercise.) Then, have the students reassemble as a class. Take the best solution choice from each group. (Use page 21 for this exercise.) Let the class vote on the top solution and give a special sticker to the team with the winning solution.

Teacher Directions *(cont.)*

7. **Let's Learn to Live Together:** Have the students follow the directions on page 22 to make badges. You may first wish to copy the badges onto colored paper and then laminate them for durability.

   For pages 23 and 24, have the students follow the directions on the pages. They can turn in page 24 at the end of the week, earning stickers or other small prizes if they have positive checklists. If they do not have positive checklists, discuss the problems and let the students try again for the following week.

   To complete the activity on page 25, the students may use the encyclopedia for reference. For example, they may need to look at world flags to get ideas for their own. Remind the students that a street can be called boulevard, road, lane, way, avenue, place, and so forth. They can also have a varied combination of cardinal directions. Stores, libraries, shops, theaters, and gas stations can have special names, and some examples are given in the directions. Let the students use their imaginations.

8. **Secret Mission: The Year of the Child:** Give each student a signed copy of the information letter on page 26, and then tell the students that the S.A.V. club has decided to make this year "The Year of the Child." That means that the members must think of ways to keep children safe and sound. The students will complete each activity sheet (pages 27, 28, 29, and 30) either as a written assignment or orally to the whole class. You can assign the approach you would prefer, such as a play or skit for one theme and a cooperative learning activity for another. Each theme heading for pages 27-30 can then be made into a banner for a bulletin board. Display the students' papers and drawings on the board.

   To complete page 31, follow the directions on the page. Allow the students to use a dictionary, if desired.

9. **Literature: The Berenstain Bears:** Read *The Berenstain Bears Get in a Fight* by Stan and Jan Berenstain. Use the vocabulary and discussion questions (page 32), if desired. The students should then complete one of the story maps (pages 33, 34, and 35) as an independent activity, or the teacher may complete a story map with the class.

   The book report form on page 36 is for younger students to use with the Berenstain Bears book; however, older students should be required to read a book on their own. They may read a book about the life and work of an important peacemaker, such as Martin Luther King, Jr. or Gandhi, or any story about conflicts and peaceful resolutions. Check with your school librarian for suggestions.

   Use the bookmarks on page 37 for rewards or just for pleasure. The students can color their own bookmarks. Laminate them for the students, if possible.

Teacher Directions *(cont.)*

10. **Creative Writing:** Give each student a copy of page 38. Have them pick a story starter to use, or let them choose one story starter per week. Beginning students can simply write one or two sentences and illustrate them.

11. **The Writing Process:** Review each step of the writing process with your students, using the information provided on page 39. Have the students pair together and then pick one of the following topics:

    - What is the S.A.V. club?
    - Why are gangs wrong?
    - Why are drugs harmful?
    - How can we stop violence?

    The partners will work together on an essay about their chosen topic. Partner teams may help other partner teams when prewriting, revising, and proofreading.

12. **Encyclopedia Search:** Tell your students that they have been promoted to Fight Buster Investigators (F.B.I.). Then, follow the directions on page 40.

13. **Secret Language:** Children love to use sign language. Let them use the sign language alphabet (page 41) to spell "hugs, not slugs," their secret password phrase. They can also use the alphabet to spell other positive words and messages.

14. **Word Scramble:** Follow the directions on page 42.

15. **Newspaper Reporter:** Here is a great way to enforce the concept of nonviolence and to teach good writing skills. Review the five W's (who, what, where, when, and why) with the class. Allow them to choose one headline from page 43. Tell them they must submit their stories to you by the end of the week. Read the stories aloud to the class.

    If it is possible, you should start your own S.A.V. club newsletter. Collect stories of positive student behavior during the month. Assign several students to be the reporters who will write the stories. Then, publish those stories in your newsletter. You can use the form on page 44 or create your own. If you are unable to produce a newsletter for your class, ask to have a column in the school's newsletter.

16. **Student and Teacher Conference:** All S.A.V. members receive "private consultations" with the Fight Buster Instructor (the teacher). Make this an opportunity to boost self-esteem while correcting inappropriate behaviors. Use the form on page 45.

17. **Poster Contest:** Allow students to work in groups to design peace posters (page 46) that specifically deal with antiviolence. Let the students vote on the best posters. Award the winners a special treat, such as stickers or extra free time. Display the posters in your room or hallway.

18. **Special Diploma:** At the completion of this unit, have a special day or party. Award each student a diploma (page 47).

S.A.V. Membership Cards

Join the secret Students Against Violence (S.A.V.) club. You will get a special and private membership card. You can make a briefcase to store all your S.A.V. documents. You will learn a secret rap song. Plus, there are contracts, rewards, a poster contest, and much more.

To begin, color and cut out your membership card. You and your teacher will sign your names. Fold the card in half to make it stand on your desk or table, or keep your card in your S.A.V. briefcase.

(Place reward stickers below.)

This is to certify that the student listed on this card has all the rights, privileges, and responsibilities that go with membership in the S.A.V. club.

- -

S.A.V. Membership Card

(Students Against Violence)

_____
Name

_____
Teacher

Contract

Students Against Violence

I, _____, agree to abide by all the rules of the S.A.V. club. I will not fight with, bite, or push anyone. I will keep my hands to myself. I promise not to talk in a mean or unkind way. I will speak kindly, and I will work cooperatively with others. I also promise to do all I can to stop violence. I want to be a Student Against Violence.

_____
S.A.V. member signature

_____
F.B.I. (Fight Buster Instructor) signature

Briefcase

This is a special briefcase for S.A.V. members. Keep all your important documents inside.

Materials:

12" x 18" (30 cm x 45 cm) sheet of construction paper (any color)

4½" x 6" (11.25 cm x 15 cm) sheet of construction paper (same color as above)

- scissors
- glue
- crayons or markers (optional)
- stickers (optional)

Directions:

1. Fold the larger sheet of construction paper twice, as shown.

2. Glue the lower edges together to form a pocket.

3. Fold the smaller sheet of paper in half, as shown.

4. To make a handle, cut away the center of the smaller paper without cutting the fold.

5. Glue the loose ends of the handle to the top of the larger construction paper.

6. To make a latch, trim a construction paper scrap to the desired size and glue the lower half of the latch to the lower portion of the briefcase. To close the briefcase, simply tuck in the upper fold, as shown.

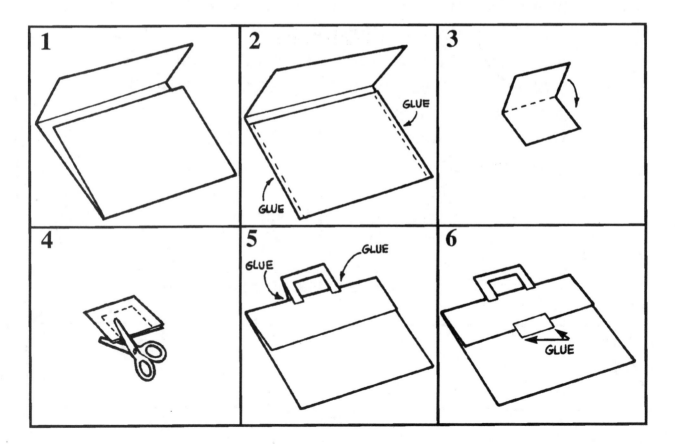

Word Web

Listen to your teacher for directions.

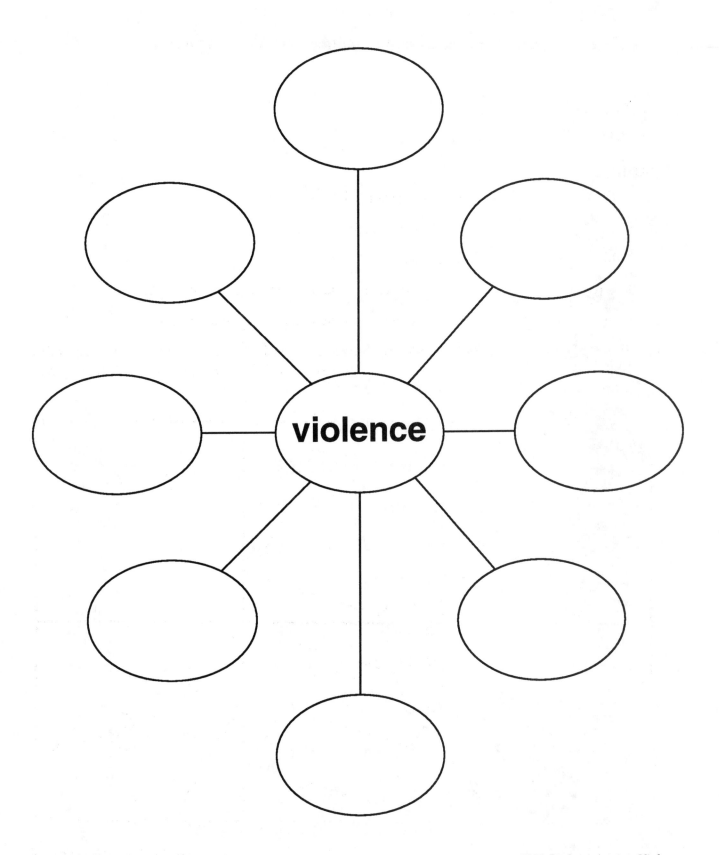

Hugs, Not Slugs

Hugs, not slugs
Is what we say.
We are kind
In every way.
We do our best.
We are good.
We solve our problems
Like we should.
We never fight.
We never bite.
We always share.
We do what's right.
So if you want
To join our club,
Just remember,
Hugs, not slugs!

Cloze Activity

Use the words in the word bank to fill in the correct missing words in the rap.

Hugs, not _____,is what we say. We are

_____ in every way. We do our _____.

We are _____. We _____

our _____ like we should. We never fight.

We never _____. We always _____.

We do what's right. So if you want to join our _____,

just remember, _____,not slugs!

Word Bank

problems	share
hugs	solve
best	bite
good	club
slugs	kind

Handwriting Practice

Write the "Hugs, Not Slugs" rap in your best handwriting. Hang the rap in your room or in some special place.

_____

_____

_____

_____

_____

_____

_____

_____

_____

_____

_____

_____

_____

_____

_____

ABC Order

Put the words from the word bank in ABC order. All of the words can be found in the rap, "Hugs, Not Slugs."

Word Bank

right	hugs	kind
solve	club	join
best	we	good
share	remember	want

---

1. _____

2. _____

3. _____

4. _____

5. _____

6. _____

7. _____

8. _____

9. _____

10. _____

11. _____

12. _____

Bonus: Use these words to write four funny sentences on the back of this paper.

What Do They Mean?

1. kind

2. solve

3. join

4. good

5. share

6. club

7. best

Dictionary Skills

Put the words from the word bank on the correct page of the dictionary.

Word Bank

violence	friendly	excellent	slugs
problems	caring	hugs	best
share	punch	kindness	bite
positive	solve	goodness	cooperative
club	pleasant		

A - H   **I - Z**

Bonus: On the back of this paper, put all of the words in ABC order.

Multiple Meanings

Many words have more than one meaning. With a partner, use a dictionary to find the different meanings of the words below. Then, on the back of this paper, write a sentence using each definition.

Word	Definitions
1. slug	
2. punch	
3. solution	
4. mean	
5. rap	
6. play	
7. hit	

16

Make a Word

Use the letters in the word "peaceful" to make as many different words as possible. For each word, use a letter only as many times as that letter appears in "peaceful." For example, you could not use the word "apple" because it needs two P's.

Peaceful

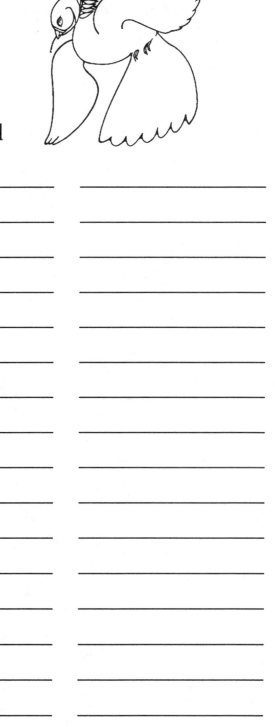

_____   _____   _____

_____   _____   _____

_____   _____   _____

_____   _____   _____

_____   _____   _____

_____   _____   _____

_____   _____   _____

_____   _____   _____

_____   _____   _____

_____   _____   _____

_____   _____   _____

_____   _____   _____

_____   _____   _____

_____   _____   _____

Synonym Search

Find as many synonyms as you can for the word "peaceful." Write them in the word web below.

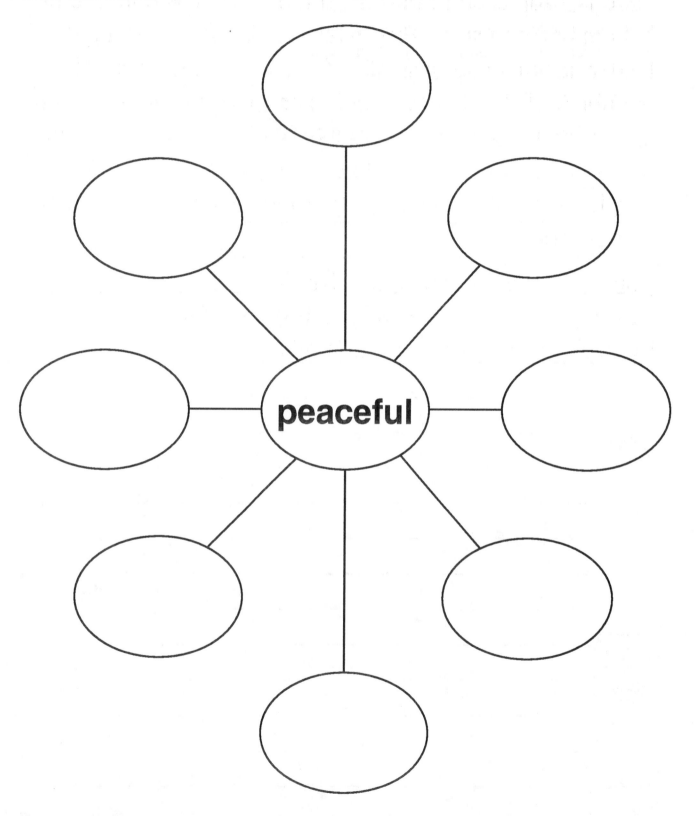

Can You Solve a Mystery?

Here is a top secret mission, and only S.A.V. club members may try to solve this mystery. A top government leader has made an urgent call for help. She wants the members of the S.A.V. to help her solve a mystery. First, she wants to know who is causing all the violence around us. Second, she wants to know what to do about it. Your mission (should you decide to accept it) is to answer her two questions.

You will work in teams to solve this mystery. Your Fight Buster Instructor will give you further information. Remember, this is a top secret mission!

Good luck,

_____

F.B.I.
(Fight Buster Instructor)

Our Solutions

Group: _____

Names: _____

_____

_____

_____

_____

List three solutions:

1.

2.

3.

Vote for the best solution.

20

Best Solutions

List each group's choice for the best solution. Then, as a class, vote for the best solution of all. Circle the winner.

Group A:

Group B:

Group C:

Group D:

Group E:

Let's Learn to Live Together

Color and cut out your badge. Then, use scissors to cut a slit at the top. Attach the badge to a button on your shirt or blouse or hook it on with a safety pin. Wearing this badge shows that you are committed to living peacefully.

Crack the Code

To find the secret message you will have to crack the code. Can you do it?
Give it a try!

A	B	C	D	E	F	G	H	I	J	K	L	M
1	2	3	4	5	6	7	8	9	10	11	12	13
N	O	P	Q	R	S	T	U	V	W	X	Y	Z
14	15	16	17	18	19	20	21	22	23	24	25	26

<pre>
___ ___ ___ ___ ,   ___ ___ ___ ___ ___
12   5   20   19   12   5   1   18   14

___ ___   ___ ___ ___ ___
20   15   12   9   22   5

___ ___ ___ ___ ___ ___ ___ ___   ___ ___
20   15   7   5   20   8   5   18   9   14

___ ___ ___ ___ ___   ___ ___ ___
16   5   1   3   5   1   14   4

___ ___ ___ ___ ___ ___ ___ !
8   1   18   13   15   14   25
</pre>

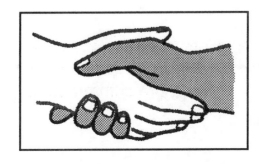

Checklist

Read this list. Try to do these things every day. At the end of the week, check one of the boxes to show how you have done.

Behavior	True	False
I spoke kindly to other students.		
I played safely and fairly on the playground.		
I listened to my teacher.		
I did not watch violence on television, movies, or video games.		
I did not push or hit another student.		
I did not tease another student.		
I shared when I could.		
I always tried my best.		

Make a Better World

As a member of the S.A.V. club, you have an opportunity to make the world a better place to live. So, instead of complaining, take action and imagine a place that is safe and happy.

Your imaginary country will be called S.A.V. You and your teammates will figure out the rest of the information. Follow the directions below.

1. Name your cities (ex: Lovesville, Togethertown, and Hugsburg).

2. Name your streets (ex: Love Lane, Peaceful Avenue, and Positive Place).

3. Design a flag that represents your country.

4. Draw a map of your city, showing the streets, buildings, and stores. Label your map. Make a map key.

5. Name your stores and buildings (ex: Friend Builders, a business that helps people to make friends).

6. Write a history of your country. Answer the five w's: who, what, when, where, and why. (Ask your Fight Buster Instructor to explain these further if you need more information.)

7. Turn in your assignment to the F.B.I. by _____.

Secret Mission: The Year of the Child

This mission is for S.A.V. members only! The S.A.V. club has decided to make this year The Year of the Child. Your mission is to find ways that children can be safe and sound all year round. You can accomplish this by completing the following activity sheets. Do your best, and good luck!

F.B.I. _____

(Fight Buster Instructor)

Sign below if you are ready to accept this mission.

_____

F.B.I.

(Fight Buster Investigator)

I Can Cope—
I Don't Need Dope!

Complete these sentences.

1. I can cope because... _____

_____

2. When I am afraid, I can... _____

_____

3. When I need money, I can... _____

_____

4. When I see drugs around me, I can... _____

_____

5. When I am curious about drugs, I can... _____

_____

6. When I am sad, I can... _____

_____

7. When I am angry, I can... _____

_____

I Know How to Handle "Stranger Danger"

Complete these sentences.

1. If someone I do not know offers me candy, I will...

   _____

   _____

   _____

2. If someone I do not know asks me to take a ride with him/her, I will...

   _____

   _____

   _____

3. If someone I do not know chases me, I will...

   _____

   _____

   _____

4. If someone I do not know touches me, I will...

   _____

   _____

   _____

I'm Home Alone but Acting Grown

Complete the following story.

Jasmine was home alone. As she sat watching her favorite television show, someone knocked loudly on the door. Jasmine looked out the window to see who it was. She did not know the man standing there. "Who is it?" she called out nervously.

"I'm a friend. Your mother sent me. Please open the door," said the man in a low whisper.

Jasmine thought for a moment. Then she _____

_____

_____

_____

_____

_____

_____

_____

_____

Get a Grip! Gangs Aren't Hip

Answer the questions. Tell why you chose your answers.

1. What does it mean to be violent?

   _____

   _____

2. Is it a good idea to join a gang? _____

   _____

   _____

3. Is it wrong to hurt other people?

   _____

   _____

4. Why is it dangerous to have a gun?

   _____

   _____

5. Is it okay to hit someone because you are angry?

   _____

   _____

Favorite Words

Here are two favorite words of the S.A.V. See if you can write a positive word for each letter.

P _____

E _____

A _____

C _____

E _____

F _____

U _____

L _____

F _____

R _____

I _____

E _____

N _____

D _____

L _____

Y _____

Literature: The Berenstain Bears

Review the vocabulary words below and look up the definition for any word you do not know. Then, read *The Berenstain Bears Get in a Fight* , (Random, 1988) Discuss the story, using these questions.

1. What causes the fight between the cubs?

2. What do the cubs do when they get angry?

3. Can the cubs remember what they had been fighting about?

4. How do the cubs finally solve their problems?

5. Is it normal for people to argue?

Vocabulary Words		
nicely	together	mood
racket	shouted	fight
snapped	foolish	snarled
angry	mean	argument

Story Map I

Title:

Author:

Setting:

Characters:

---

1. What is the problem?

---

2. How is the problem solved?

---

3. What did you learn from this story?

Story Map II

Vocabulary	Sequence of Events
	First
	Next
	Then
	Last

34

Story Map III

Title:	
Setting:	
Main Idea:	
Characters:	

What happens in the story?
First
Next
Then
Last

What problem is in the story?
How is the problem solved?

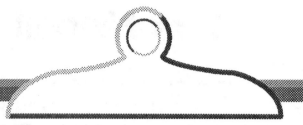

F.B.I. Book Report

Here is a special book report form for all Fight Buster Investigators.

Title:

Author:

Illustrator:

Publisher:

Number of Pages:

Setting:

Main Character(s):

Fiction: _____ **Nonfiction:** _____

Plot:

Favorite Part:

Signed,

_____

F.B.I.

Bookmarks

Let's Learn to Live Together

_____
Name

S.A.V.

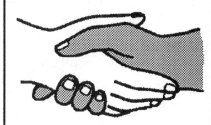

Students
Against
Violence

_____
Name

HUGS,

NOT SLUGS

_____
Name

Creative Writing

Choose one of the prompts below and write a paragraph.

If I were Superman, I would help others by…

_____

_____

_____

_____

People should not fight because…

_____

_____

_____

_____

We should forgive others because…

_____

_____

_____

_____

If someone wants me to join a gang, I will tell him/her…

_____

_____

_____

_____

The Writing Process

Step 1: Think Tank *(Prewriting)*

- Think about what you want to say.
- Brainstorm and list related words and your thoughts.

Step 2: Fast Draft *(First Draft)*

- Write what you want to say.
- Do not worry about spelling or grammar.

Step 3: Revision Decision *(Revising)*

- Think about what you wrote.
- Take words out or add new words.
- Be sure you have written complete sentences.

Step 4: Check and Correct *(Proofreading)*

- Check your spelling, grammar, and punctuation.
- Let your partner check your work.

Step 5: Perfect Paper *(Final Draft)*

- Copy your paper in your best handwriting.
- Turn in your paper to the teacher or display it.
- Read your paper aloud to the class.
- Place your paper in your briefcase.

Encyclopedia Search

You have been promoted to the level of F.B.I. super-agent. Your first major assignment is to look up "gang" in an encyclopedia. You need to know all you can before you can effectively fight violence! Take notes about what you read. Then, write down the information by following the five w's (who, what, where, when, and why). Turn in your report to the Fight Buster Instructor on _____. Get going, and good luck!

_____

_____

_____

_____

_____

_____

_____

_____

_____

_____

_____

_____

_____

Secret Language

All Fight Buster Investigators need a secret language. Use the sign alphabet to spell "hugs, not slugs." From now on, this is the secret password phrase for all S.A.V. club members.

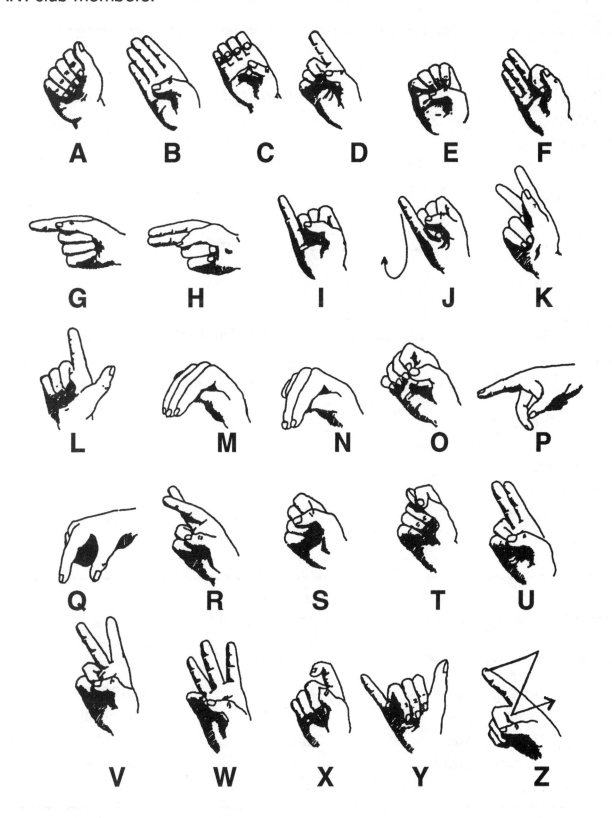

Word Scramble

Since you have been promoted to the level of F.B.I. super-agent, you have another assignment. The words below are scrambled. Only S.A.V. members may know what they are. See if you can unscramble them. As always, good luck!

_____
F.B.I. (Fight Buster Instructor)

1. gslus _____

2. vsleo _____

3. suhg _____

4. ebit _____

5. bcul _____

6. ocporetavie _____

7. yflrdine _____

8. gcnair _____

9. opstivie _____

10. sksiendn _____

11. rhsae _____

12. steb _____

13. sgosdone _____

14. rpboelsm _____

15. lpaeastn _____

16. ivloneec _____

17. tenxeclel _____

18. upcnh _____

Word Bank

slugs	friendly	goodness
solve	caring	problems
hugs	positive	violence
bite	kindness	excellent
club	share	punch
cooperative	best	pleasant

Newspaper Reporter

Memo

To: Fight Buster Investigators

From: Fight Buster Instructor

Date: _____

Subject: Newspaper Story

As a Fight Buster Investigator, you have the scoop on a hot story — "No More Violence!" You decide to be the first to publish the news. Pick one of the headlines below or use your own headline. Then, begin writing. Remember to include the five w's in your story: who, what, when, where, and why. You can use the form on the next page or create your own.

Headlines

"NO MORE GANGS!"

"VIOLENCE CEASES!"

"KIDS REFUSE TO FIGHT!"

"FRIENDS, NOT FOES!!"

Newspaper Reporter *(cont.)*

_____
Newspaper

_____   _____   _____
City   Date   Cost

| Headline | Photo or Illustration |

Student and Teacher Conference

Date: _____

I had a conference with my teacher today. Here are my good points.

Here are some things I need to work on.

Student: _____

Teacher: _____

Poster Contest

Hey Kids,

Enter the "Hugs, Not Slugs" poster contest. Design your own special poster. Follow these directions:

1. Use an 11½" x 14" (29 cm x 35 cm) sheet of paper or poster board.

2. Draw a picture to illustrate your poster.

3. Write a phrase or sentence that opposes violence.

4. Make your poster interesting with a good message. Remember, you are competing in a contest.

Turn in your poster to the Fight Buster Instructor by _____ .

Special Diploma

To _____

for working so hard to stop violence.

You are a special person!

Signed,

_____
Fight Buster Instructor

Answer Key

Page 11
slugs
kind
best
good
solve
problems
bite
share
club
hugs

Page 13
best
club
good
hugs
join
kind
remember
right
share
solve
want
we

Page 14
Answers will vary.

Page 15

A-H	I – Z
best	kindness
bite	pleasant
caring	positive
club	problems
cooperative	punch
excellent	share
friendly	slugs
goodness	solve
hugs	violence

Page 16
Answers will vary.

Page 17
Following is a partial list of words: a, ace, ape, cafe, calf, cap, cape, clap, cup, eel, face, fee, feel, flap, flea, flee, flu, flue, fuel, lace, lap, leaf, leap, lee, pace, pal, pale, pea, peace, peel, place, plea, up

Page 23
Let's learn to live together in peace and harmony!

Page 42
1. slugs
2. solve
3. hugs
4. bite
5. club
6. cooperative
7. friendly
8. caring
9. positive
10. kindness
11. share
12. best
13. goodness
14. problems
15. pleasant
16. violence
17. excellent
18. punch